Little People, **BIG DREAMS**™

LOUIS PASTEUR

Written by
Maria Isabel Sánchez Vegara

Illustrated by
Shelly Laslo

Frances Lincoln
Children's Books

Little Louis was born in France at a time when doctors didn't know much about why people got sick. Most of the time, they used odd and painful cures that didn't even work. But luckily for Louis, he grew up strong and healthy.

From an early age, he showed a natural talent for drawing and painted beautiful portraits of his parents and friends.

Yet, when he was a teen, he discovered his love for science and went on to study at some of the best colleges in his country.

Louis was a teacher at the University of Strasbourg when he met Marie, his lifelong love. After they got married, they moved to Lille, where Monsieur Bigot, the father of one of his students, begged Louis to find out why his wine was spoiling.

Other scientists had already discovered little organisms
called microbes. They were so little that they could only
be seen using a microscope, but they were everywhere:
in the air, in water… even in Monsieur Bigot's wine!

After Louis proved that microbes were damaging the wine, the Emperor of France urged him to go back to his lab and find a way to get rid of these unwanted guests. It was not an easy task, but Louis was eager to try his best.

Louis found out that microbes could be killed by heating up the wine. He called his process "pasteurization," a method that is still used today to make things like milk, cheese, or juice last longer.

The Academy of Sciences offered a prize to anyone who could prove where microbes came from. Louis won by showing that they didn't appear from nowhere—as many believed—but came from other living beings. It was a major step for science!

By that time, three of his children had died from a disease called typhoid. Louis promised himself that he would put all of his efforts into preventing other kids from dying, too.

He thought that if microbes could spoil food,
they could also cause diseases.

He turned his lab into a farm to study animal diseases such as chicken cholera. One day, his assistant Charles injected weak microbes into their feathered patients by mistake.

The chickens fell sick, but their disease
was milder than usual.

Louis decided to expose the chickens to the microbes again, but using a stronger dose. Luckily for the chickens, their bodies recognized the tiny invaders and fought back, winning the battle against the disease.

That was the first vaccine created in a laboratory, and soon Louis was ready to try it on humans. When he vaccinated a little boy bitten by a rabid dog, Louis didn't just save his life: he changed the course of medicine forever.

Louis became the most renowned scientist in the world.
From his institute, he opened the door for others to create
new vaccines.

These vaccines saved millions of lives and stopped
the spread of many diseases that had terrified people
for centuries.

And science will forever be thankful to little Louis:
the father of microbiology and the restless dreamer
who solved one of life's biggest mysteries by
exploring the tiniest living beings in nature.

LOUIS PASTEUR

(Born 1822 – Died 1895)

1852

1885

Louis Pasteur grew up in the town of Arbois in France. The family weren't wealthy but they were determined to provide a good education for their son. Louis earned two degrees, including a Bachelor of Science degree at the Royal College of Besançon in 1842. He met his wife, Marie, when he became a professor of chemistry at the University of Strasbourg. They had five children together, but, sadly, only two survived childhood as the others fell ill to infectious diseases. After moving to Lille, Louis was asked to find out why bottles of wine were spoiling. He soon realized that tiny microbes were responsible for souring the wine. He invented a process in which bacteria could be removed by boiling and then cooling liquid. Today, this is known as pasteurization. Louis went on to make some vital discoveries

1889

c. 1891

as he researched a disease called chicken cholera. After chickens were
accidentally exposed to a weakened form of the illness, Louis found that
they became resistant to it. On July 6, 1885, Louis successfully vaccinated
Joseph Meister, a young boy who had been bitten by a rabid dog.
The era of preventive medicine moved rapidly and Louis became one
of the most famous scientists across the world. In 1888, he opened the
Pasteur Institute in Paris, bringing together other scientists to search for
even more breakthroughs to help humankind. Louis is remembered
for his life-changing contributions to medicine. His research has been
used by other scientists to develop vaccinations for human diseases such
as tuberculosis and smallpox, saving millions of lives across the world.

Want to find out more about **Louis Pasteur?**

Have a read of this great book:

Louis Pasteur: Genius by Jane Kent and Isabel Munoz

If you're in Paris, France, you can visit the Pasteur Museum.

Brimming with creative inspiration, how-to projects, and useful information to enrich your everyday life, quarto.com is a favorite destination for those pursuing their interests and passions.

Text © 2023 Maria Isabel Sánchez Vegara. Illustrations © 2023 Shelly Laslo.
"Little People, BIG DREAMS" and "Pequeña & Grande" are trademarks of
Alba Editorial S.L.U. and/or Beautifool Couple S.L.
First Published in the UK in 2023 by Frances Lincoln Children's Books, an imprint of The Quarto Group.
100 Cummings Center, Suite 265D, Beverly, MA 01915, USA
T +1 978-282-9590 www.Quarto.com

This book is not authorised, licensed or approved by the estate of Louis Pasteur.
Any faults are the publisher's who will be happy to rectify for future printings.
A CIP record for this book is available from the Library of Congress.
ISBN 978-0-7112-8313-8
Set in Futura BT.

Published by Peter Marley • Designed by Sasha Moxon
Commissioned by Lucy Menzies • Edited by Lucy Menzies and Rachel Robinson
Production by Nikki Ingram
Manufactured in Guangdong, China CC112022
1 3 5 7 9 8 6 4 2

Photographic acknowledgements (pages 28-29, from left to right): 1. Portrait of Louis Pasteur (1822-1895), 1852, France © Photo 12 via Getty Images. 2. Louis Pasteur, (1822-1895), in his laboratory, portrait painting by Albert Edelfelt, 1885 © incamerastock via Alamy Photos. 3. LOUIS PASTEUR (1822-1895). /French chemist and microbiologist. Photographed by Nadar in 1889 © GRANGER – Historical Picture Archive via Alamy Photos. 4. French scientist Louis Pasteur (1822 - 1895), father of modern bacteriology, circa 1891 © PictureLux/The Hollywood Archive via Alamy Photos

Collect the Little People, BIG DREAMS™ series:

| FRIDA KAHLO | COCO CHANEL | MAYA ANGELOU | AMELIA EARHART | AGATHA CHRISTIE | MARIE CURIE | ROSA PARKS | AUDREY HEPBURN |

| EMMELINE PANKHURST | ELLA FITZGERALD | ADA LOVELACE | JANE AUSTEN | GEORGIA O'KEEFFE | HARRIET TUBMAN | ANNE FRANK | MOTHER TERESA |

| JOSEPHINE BAKER | L. M. MONTGOMERY | JANE GOODALL | SIMONE DE BEAUVOIR | MUHAMMAD ALI | STEPHEN HAWKING | MARIA MONTESSORI | VIVIENNE WESTWOOD |

| MAHATMA GANDHI | DAVID BOWIE | WILMA RUDOLPH | DOLLY PARTON | BRUCE LEE | RUDOLF NUREYEV | ZAHA HADID | MARY SHELLEY |

| MARTIN LUTHER KING JR. | DAVID ATTENBOROUGH | ASTRID LINDGREN | EVONNE GOOLAGONG | BOB DYLAN | ALAN TURING | BILLIE JEAN KING | GRETA THUNBERG |

| JESSE OWENS | JEAN-MICHEL BASQUIAT | ARETHA FRANKLIN | CORAZON AQUINO | PELÉ | ERNEST SHACKLETON | STEVE JOBS | AYRTON SENNA |

| LOUISE BOURGEOIS | ELTON JOHN | JOHN LENNON | PRINCE | CHARLES DARWIN | CAPTAIN TOM MOORE | HANS CHRISTIAN ANDERSEN | STEVIE WONDER |

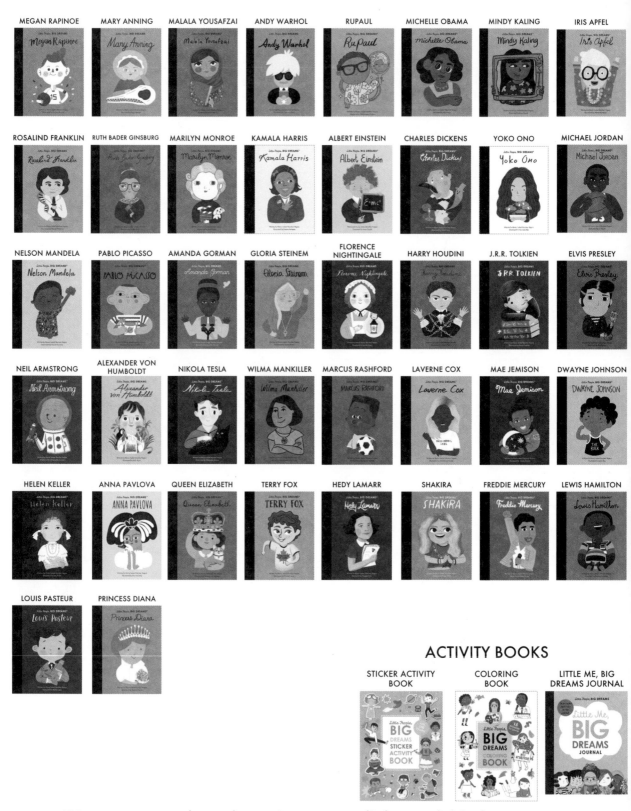

MEGAN RAPINOE   MARY ANNING   MALALA YOUSAFZAI   ANDY WARHOL   RUPAUL   MICHELLE OBAMA   MINDY KALING   IRIS APFEL

ROSALIND FRANKLIN   RUTH BADER GINSBURG   MARILYN MONROE   KAMALA HARRIS   ALBERT EINSTEIN   CHARLES DICKENS   YOKO ONO   MICHAEL JORDAN

NELSON MANDELA   PABLO PICASSO   AMANDA GORMAN   GLORIA STEINEM   FLORENCE NIGHTINGALE   HARRY HOUDINI   J.R.R. TOLKIEN   ELVIS PRESLEY

NEIL ARMSTRONG   ALEXANDER VON HUMBOLDT   NIKOLA TESLA   WILMA MANKILLER   MARCUS RASHFORD   LAVERNE COX   MAE JEMISON   DWAYNE JOHNSON

HELEN KELLER   ANNA PAVLOVA   QUEEN ELIZABETH   TERRY FOX   HEDY LAMARR   SHAKIRA   FREDDIE MERCURY   LEWIS HAMILTON

LOUIS PASTEUR   PRINCESS DIANA

ACTIVITY BOOKS

STICKER ACTIVITY BOOK   COLORING BOOK   LITTLE ME, BIG DREAMS JOURNAL

Discover more about the series at www.littlepeoplebigdreams.com